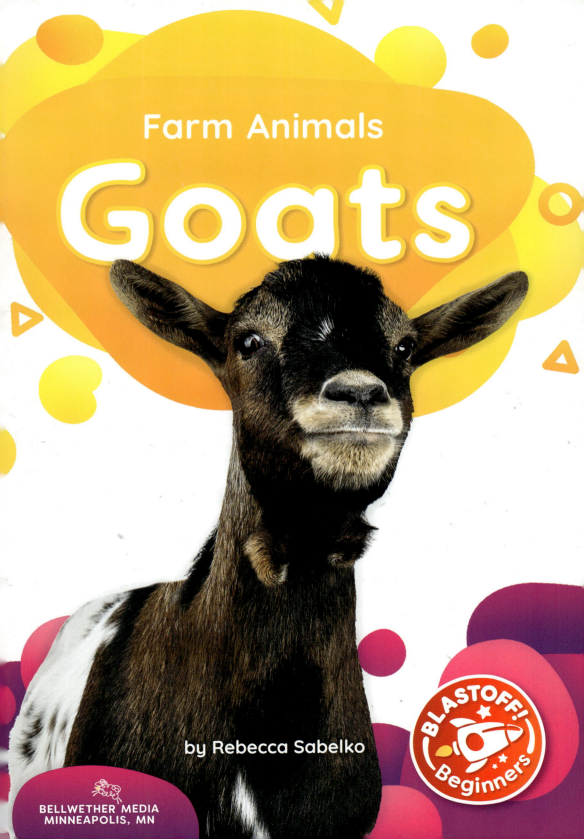

Blastoff! Beginners are developed by literacy experts and educators to meet the needs of early readers. These engaging informational texts support young children as they begin reading about their world. Through simple language and high frequency words paired with crisp, colorful photos, Blastoff! Beginners launch young readers into the universe of independent reading.

Sight Words in This Book

a	find	jump	run	to
and	have	like	some	too
be	help	little	these	
big	in	many	they	
can	is	may	this	
eat	it	play	time	

This edition first published in 2024 by Bellwether Media, Inc.

No part of this publication may be reproduced in whole or in part without written permission of the publisher. For information regarding permission, write to Bellwether Media, Inc., Attention: Permissions Department, 6012 Blue Circle Drive, Minnetonka, MN 55343.

Library of Congress Cataloging-in-Publication Data

Names: Sabelko, Rebecca, author.
Title: Goats / by Rebecca Sabelko.
Description: Minneapolis, MN : Bellwether Media, 2024. | Series: Blastoff! Beginners: Farm Animals | Includes bibliographical references and index. | Audience: Ages 4-7 | Audience: Grades K-1
Identifiers: LCCN 2023039755 (print) | LCCN 2023039756 (ebook) | ISBN 9798886877618 (library binding) | ISBN 9798886879490 (paperback) | ISBN 9798886878554 (ebook)
Subjects: LCSH: Goats--Juvenile literature.
Classification: LCC SF383.35 .S23 2024 (print) | LCC SF383.35 (ebook) | DDC 636.3/9--dc23/eng/20230831
LC record available at https://lccn.loc.gov/2023039755
LC ebook record available at https://lccn.loc.gov/2023039756

Text copyright © 2024 by Bellwether Media, Inc. BLASTOFF! BEGINNERS and associated logos are trademarks and/or registered trademarks of Bellwether Media, Inc.

Editor: Elizabeth Neuenfeldt   Designer: Laura Sowers

Printed in the United States of America, North Mankato, MN.

Table of Contents

Time to Play!	4
What Are Goats?	6
Life on the Farm	12
Goat Facts	22
Glossary	23
To Learn More	24
Index	24

Time to Play!

Goats like to play. They **butt** heads!

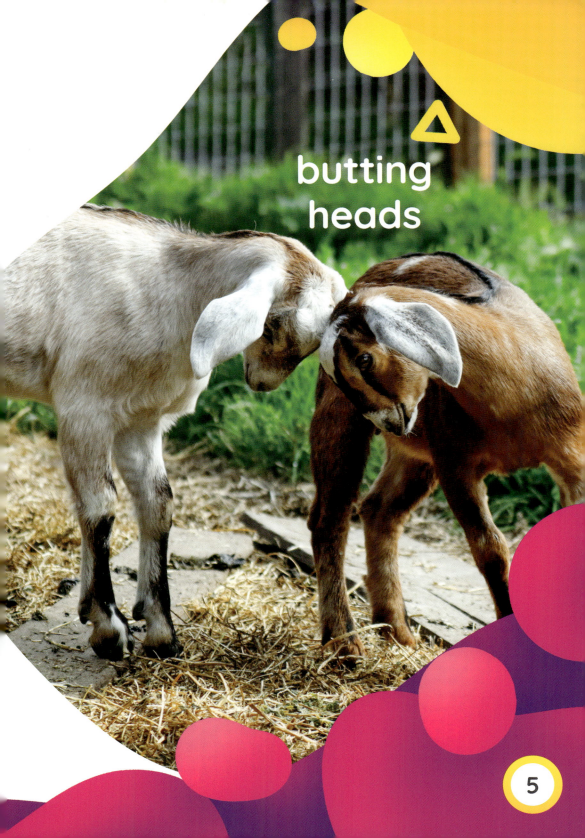
butting heads

What Are Goats?

Goats can be big or little. They can be many colors.

Goats can have **horns**. Some have a **beard**.

beard

Goats have **split hooves**. These help goats run and jump.

split hooves

Life on the Farm

Goats often live in barns. They live in sheds, too.

shed

They also spend time in fields. They find food.

field

Goats eat many plants! They like hay and weeds.

hay

hay

weeds

Female goats may give milk.

milk

This goat
is hungry.
It is time to eat.
Meh, meh!

Goat Facts

Parts of a Goat

horns

beard

spilt hooves

Life on the Farm

butt heads   find food   give milk

22

Glossary

beard — a group of long hairs on the necks of some goats

butt — to hit with the top of the head

horns — hard parts on the heads of some goats

split hooves — hard foot coverings that have two parts

To Learn More

ON THE WEB

FACTSURFER

Factsurfer.com gives you a safe, fun way to find more information.

1. Go to www.factsurfer.com.
2. Enter "goats" into the search box and click 🔍.
3. Select your book cover to see a list of related content.

Index

barns, 12, 13
beard, 8
butt heads, 4, 5
colors, 6
eat, 16, 20
female, 18
fields, 14, 15
food, 14, 16, 17

hay, 16, 17
horns, 8, 9
jump, 10
milk, 18
plants, 16
play, 4
run, 10
sheds, 12
size, 6

split hooves, 10
weeds, 16, 17

The images in this book are reproduced through the courtesy of: Nynke van Holten, cover; Eric Isselee, pp. 3, 9; Rita_Kochmarjova, pp. 4, 6, 10-11; GoDog Photo, pp. 4-5; Thep Photos, pp. 6-7; DrPAS, p. 8; Kummeleon, p. 10; André Muller, p. 12; Ten03, pp. 12-13; Prism Acres Rebecca Young, p. 14; ilkah, pp. 14-15; Sportactive, pp. 16-17; Oleksiichik, p. 17 (hay); Orest Iyzhechka, p. 17 (weeds); Sarah Marchant, p. 18; EarlyDawnPhotography2, pp. 18-19; egon69, pp. 20-21; photomaster, p. 22; Saga Photo and Video, p. 22 (butt heads); Dudarev Mikhail, p. 22 (find food); LiAndStudio, p. 22 (give milk); Dmitry Kalinovsky, p. 23 (beard); Thomas Dekiere, p. 23 (butt); tanitost, p. 23 (horns); schankz, p. 23 (split hooves).